Quick-to-Solve
Brainteasers

Official
American Mensa
puzzle book

J.J. Mendoza Fernández

D0981394

Sterling Publishing Co., Inc.
New York

English version edited by Peter Gordon.

Translated from Spanish by Natalia M. Tizón.

Clip art for puzzles 110, 159, and 224 from Federal Clip Art,
www.onemileup.com. All other clip art from Corel.

Library of Congress Cataloging-in-Publication Data Available

10 9 8 7 6 5 4

Published by Sterling Publishing Company, Inc.
387 Park Avenue South, New York, N.Y. 10016
Originally published in Argentina and Spain by
Juegos & Co., S.R.L. and Zugarto Ediciones
under the titles *Para Resolver en el Autobús* and *Para Resolver en el Ascensor*
© 1996 and 1997 by José Julián Mendoza Fernández
English translation © 1998 by Sterling Publishing Co., Inc.
Distributed in Canada by Sterling Publishing
℅ Canadian Manda Group, One Atlantic Avenue, Suite 105
Toronto, Ontario, Canada M6K 3E7
Distributed in Great Britain and Europe by Cassell PLC
Wellington House, 125 Strand, London WC2R 0BB, England
Distributed in Australia by Capricorn Link (Australia) Pty Ltd.
P.O. Box 6651, Baulkham Hills, Business Centre, NSW 2153, Australia

Sterling ISBN 0-8069-6151-1

CONTENTS

INTRODUCTION

This book contains many different types of puzzles: numerical puzzles, logic puzzles, word games, lateral thinking puzzles, riddles, etc. Most of them are extremely short and can be solved mentally in just a minute or two. When writing is required, a small slip of paper should be more than adequate.

The purpose of these puzzles is to entertain. The correct answer is not always obvious and this is one of the amusing aspects of this book. The reader will notice that the puzzles are often misleading or involve humor in the answer. Therefore, use your imagination, be alert, and have an open mind when trying the puzzles.

NUMBERS

0123456789

1

How many times can you subtract 6 from 30?

2

What number can you subtract half from to obtain a result that is zero?

3

How can half of 12 be 7?

4

Find two positive numbers that have a one-digit answer when multiplied and a two-digit answer when added.

5

Find two whole, positive numbers that have the same answer when multiplied together as when one is divided by the other.

6

Find two positive numbers that have the same answer when multiplied together as when added together.

7

Find a two-digit number that equals two times the result of multiplying its digits.

8

Find three whole, positive numbers that have the same answer when multiplied together as when added together.

9

What two two-digit numbers are each equal to their right-most digit squared?

10

Find the highest number that can be written with three digits.

COMPARING NUMBERS

11

The ages of a father and a son add up to 55. The father's age is the son's age reversed. How old are they?

12

How much do 10 pieces of candy cost if one thousand pieces cost $10?

13

An outlet and a light bulb cost $1.20. We know that the outlet costs $1 more than the light bulb. How much does each cost?

PERCENTAGES

14

If 75% of all women are tall, 75% are brunette, and 75% are pretty, what is the minimum percentage of tall, brunette, pretty women?

15

Thirty-two students took a nationwide exam and all the students from New York passed it. If the students from New York made up exactly 5% of the total number of the students that passed the test, how many students passed it and how many students were from New York?

16

Of the 960 people in a theater, 17% tipped 5 cents to the usher, 50% of the remaining 83% tipped 10 cents, and the rest tipped nothing. How much did the usher get?

OTHER NUMBERS

17

What must you do to make the equation below true?
81 × 9 = 801

18

There are 100 buildings along a street. A sign maker is ordered to number the buildings from 1 to 100. How many "9's" will he need?

19

How many tickets with different points of origination and destination can be sold on a bus line that travels a loop of 25 stops?

20

We know that humans have up to 100,000 hairs. In a city with more than 200,000 people, would it be possible to find two or more people with the same number of hairs?

COUNTING

21

All my ties are red except two. All my ties are blue except two. All my ties are brown except two. How many ties do I have?

22

A street that's 30 yards long has a chestnut tree every 6 yards on both sides. How many chestnut trees are on the entire street?

23

A pet shop owner is in the countryside. If he says, "one bird per olive tree," there is one bird too many. However, if he says, "two birds per olive tree," there are no birds left over. How many birds and olive trees are there?

24

In a singles tennis tournament, 111 players participated. They used a new ball for each match. When a player lost one match, he was eliminated from the tournament. How many balls did they need?

25

Peter and John had a picnic. Peter had already eaten half of the muffins when John ate half of the remaining muffins plus three more. There were no muffins left. How many muffins did they take to the picnic?

26

A shepherd says to another, "If I give you one sheep, you will have twice the number of sheep that I have, but if you give me one, we will both have the same number of sheep." How many sheep did each shepherd have?

27

If I put in one canary per cage, I have one bird too many. However, if I put in two canaries per cage, I have one cage too many. How many cages and birds do I have?

28

If 1½ sardines cost 1½ dollars, how much would 7½ sardines cost?

29

If a brick weighs 3 pounds plus ½ a brick, what's the weight of 1½ bricks?

30

If 1½ dozen sardines costs 9½ dollars, how much do 18 sardines cost?

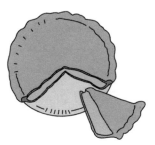

31

If 1½ men can eat 1½ pies in 1½ minutes, how many pies can 3 men eat in half an hour?

32

Yesterday afternoon, I went to visit my friend Albert, who is a painter. While I was watching him paint, I told him, "No wonder it takes you so long to finish a painting. Since I arrived, you have entered the studio twelve times." How many times did he leave the studio?

33

If two ducks are swimming in front of another duck, two ducks are swimming behind another duck, and one duck is swimming between two other ducks, what is the minimum number of ducks?

34

Two people are flipping coins. Each time, they bet $1 apiece. At the end, one person won $3 and the other one won three times. How many games did they play?

MEASURING TIME, VOLUME, LENGTH, ETC.

35

A bottle with a cylindrical shape at the bottom and with an irregular shape at the top is filled halfway to the top with liquid. The cylindrical part contains approximately three-fourths of the capacity of the bottle and we wish to determine the exact percentage of liquid that the bottle contains. We cannot open it and we can only use a ruler. What must we do?

36

If one nickel is worth five cents, how much is half of one half of a nickel worth?

37

Two soldiers have been ordered to do the following chores:

    1. Peel potatoes.

    2. Do the dishes.

    3. Mow the lawn.

Each of these chores, when done by one person, takes one hour. If they start at 8 A.M., what could they do to take as little time as possible if they have only one knife, one lawn mower, and one sink with room for one person?

38

A spider spins its web in a window frame. Each day, it spins an area equal to that of the amount already completed. It takes 30 days to cover the entire window frame. How long would two spiders take? (In the case of two spiders, each of them spins an amount equal to the area of the existing part of the web made by that particular spider.)

39

We put a spore in a test tube. Every hour the spore divides into three parts, all the same size as the original part. If we put it in at 3 P.M., at 9 P.M. the tube will be completely full. At what time will the tube be one-third full?

40

How long is a rope that is 2 yards shorter than another rope that is three times the length of the first rope?

41

If a post is 6 yards longer than half of its own length, how long is the post?

42

How much mud (measured in liters) is there in a rectangular hole 2 meters wide, 3 meters long, and 3 meters deep?

43

One mother gave 25 books to her daughter and another mother gave her daughter 8 books. However, between both daughters they only increased their collection by 25 books. How can this be?

COMPARING TIME, VOLUME, LENGTH, ETC.

44

Emily is taller than Ann and shorter than Dolores. Who is the tallest of the three?

45

Rose is now as old as Joan was six years ago. Who is older?

46

If Emily speaks in a softer voice than Ann, and Dolores in a louder voice than Ann, does Emily speak louder or softer than Dolores?

47

James is sitting between John and Peter. Philip is sitting on Peter's right. Between whom is Peter sitting?

48

What has more value, one pound of $10 gold coins or half a pound of $20 gold coins?

49

A man went into a store and bought an umbrella for $10. He gave the salesperson a $50 bill. The salesperson went to the bank to get change. Two hours later, the bank teller went to the store claiming that the $50 bill was counterfeit, so the salesperson had to exchange it for a real one with the bank teller. Between the customer and the bank, how much did the store lose?

50

We have two pitchers, one with one quart of water and the other with one quart of wine. We take a tablespoon of the wine and mix it in the pitcher of water. Then we take a tablespoon from this pitcher and mix it into the pitcher with the wine. Is there more wine in the water pitcher or more water in the wine pitcher? What would have happened if after pouring a spoonful of wine into the water, we had not mixed it well?

51

A sultan wanted to offer his daughter in marriage to the candidate whose horse would win the race. However, the rules of the race stated that the winner would be the one in last place. He didn't want the race to last forever, so he thought of a way to solve this. What was it?

WEIGHTS

52

On one side of a scale we have a partially filled fish bowl. When we put a fish in the bowl, the total weight of the bowl increases by exactly the same as the weight of the fish. However, if we hold the fish by the tail and partially introduce it into the water, will the total weight be greater than before introducing the fish?

53

We have a scale and a set of weights in a field. The scale is not very accurate, but it is consistent in its inaccuracies. How can we know the exact weight of four apples?

54

A little bird weighing 5 ounces is sleeping in a cage. We put the cage on a scale and it weighs one pound. The bird then wakes up and starts flying all over the cage. What will the scale indicate while the bird is in the air?

55

We have 10 sacks full of balls. All sacks contain balls weighing 10 ounces each, except one of the sacks, which contains balls weighing 9 ounces each. By weighing the balls, what would be the minimum number of weighings required (on a scale that gives weight readouts) to identify the sack containing the defective balls?

56

Now we have 10 sacks that contain either 10-ounce balls or 9-ounce balls. Each sack has at least 1,000 balls, and all the balls in one sack are the same weight. However, we do not know how many sacks contain the 9-ounce balls or which ones they are. How can we identify these sacks by weighing the balls (on a scale that gives weight readouts) in the fewest number of tries?

CHAINS

57

I have six pieces of a chain, each piece made up of 4 links, and I want to make a single straight chain out of them. The blacksmith charges 10 cents for cutting each link and 50 cents for welding a link. How much will the chain cost?

58

A lady arrives at a hotel where rooms are $10 per night. When she checks in, she does not have enough money, but she offers to pay with a clasped gold bracelet. The bracelet has seven links, each valued at $10. What would be the fewest number of cuts necessary to let her stay for one week if she wants to pay one day at a time?

59

"And then I took out my sword and cut the thick chain that was linked to two posts into two pieces," said the samurai.

"That is not true," said the monk.

How did the monk know the samurai's story was untrue?

MIXING

60

We have 10 glasses sitting in a row. The first five are filled with water and the other five are empty. What would be the minimum number of glasses needed to move so that the full and the empty glasses alternate?

61

In five plastic cups there are five marbles, each of different colors: white, black, red, green, and blue. We mark each cup randomly with the initial of one of the colors. If the white, green, red, and blue marbles are in their respective cups, how likely is it that the black marble is in its cup?

62

We have 8 pairs of white socks and 10 pairs of black socks in a box. What would be the minimum number of socks that we need to take out of the box to ensure that we get one pair of the same color? (Imagine that you cannot see the color when you are picking them from the box.)

63

We have 8 pairs of white socks, 9 pairs of black socks and 11 pairs of blue socks in a box. What would be the minimum number of socks that we need to take out of the box to ensure that we get one pair of the same color? (Imagine that you cannot see the color when you are picking them from the box.)

64

We have 6 pairs of white gloves and 6 pairs of black gloves in a box. What would be the minimum number of gloves that we need to take out of the box to ensure that we get one pair? (Imagine that you cannot see the color when you are picking them from the box.)

65

We have six white marbles, four black marbles, and one red marble in a box. What would be the least number of marbles that we need to take out of the box to ensure that we get three of the same color?

66

Distribute ten marbles in three plastic cups so that every cup contains an odd number of marbles. You must use all ten.

67

Distribute nine marbles in four boxes so that each box contains an odd number of marbles, different from the three other boxes. You must use all nine.

68

We have three boxes. One contains two black marbles, the second box contains two white marbles, and the third box contains one black and one white marble. The boxes are marked BB, WW, BW. However, no code corresponds with the marbles in its box. What would be the least number of marbles that must be randomly picked, from one or several boxes, to identify their contents?

CLOCKS

69

A schoolteacher uses a five-hour hourglass to keep track of class time. One day, he sets the hourglass at 9 A.M. and while he is teaching his class, a student inadvertently inverts the hourglass. Another student, who notices this, sets the hourglass to its initial position at 11:30 A.M. In this way, the class ends at 3 P.M. At what time did the first student invert the hourglass?

Quick-to-Solve Brainteasers

70

A clock gains half a minute every day. Another clock doesn't work. Which one will show the correct time more often?

71

What time is it when a clock strikes 13 times?

72

In a conventional clock, how many times does the minute hand pass the hour hand between noon and midnight?

73

If a clock takes two seconds to strike 2, how long will it take to strike 3?

74

When I gave Albert a ride home, I noticed that the clock in his living room took 7 seconds to strike 8. I immediately asked him, "How long do I have to wait to hear it strike 12?"

75

A clock takes five seconds when striking 6. How long will it take when striking 12?

CALENDAR

76

A Roman was born the first day of the 30th year before Christ and died the first day of the 30th year after Christ. How many years did he live?

77

On March 15, a friend was telling me, "Every day I have a cup of coffee. I drank 31 cups in January, 28 in February and 15 in March. So far, I drank 74 cups of coffee. Do you know how many cups I would have drunk thus far if it had been a leap year?"

78

If yesterday had been Wednesday's tomorrow and tomorrow is Sunday's yesterday, what day would today be?

79

Mrs. Smith left on a trip the day after the day before yesterday and she will be back the eve of the day after tomorrow. How many days is she away?

80

A man was telling me on a particular occasion, "The day before yesterday I was 35 years old and next year I will turn 38." How can this be?

81

A famous composer blew out 18 candles on his birthday cake and then died less than nine months later. He was 76 at the time of his death and had composed *The Barber of Seville*. How could this happen?

WORDS

82

Find a commonly used word that ends in T, contains the letters VEN, and starts with IN.

83

If you can speak properly, you will be able to answer the following question. Which is correct, "The yolk of an egg is white" or "The yolk of an egg are white"?

84

What is the opposite of "I AM NOT LEAVING"?

85

What 11-letter word is pronounced incorrectly by more than 99% of Ivy League graduates?

86

What 7-letter word becomes longer when the third letter is removed?

87

Five times four twenty, plus two, equals twenty-three. Is this true?

88

Paris starts with an "p" and ends with an "e." Is this true?

89

A phone conversation:

"May I speak to the director?"

"Who's calling?"

"John Rominch."

"I beg your pardon. Could you spell your last name?"

"R as in Rome, O as in Oslo, M as in Madrid, I as in Innsbruck ..."

"I as in what?"

"Innsbruck."

"Thanks. Please go ahead."

"N as in Nome ..."

This does not make sense. Why?

90

What can you always find in the middle of a taxicab?

91

Is the sentence "This statement is false" true or false?

92

What occurs once in June and twice in August, but never occurs in October?

93

"I must admit that I was not serious when I was telling you that I was not kidding about rethinking my decision of not changing my mind," my friend was telling me. So, is he really going to change his mind or not?

94

A criminal is sentenced to death. Before his execution, he is allowed to make a statement. If his statement is false, he will be hanged, and if his statement is true, he will be drowned. What should he say to confuse the jury and thus save his life?

COUNTING RELATIVES

95

A woman has five children and half of them are male. Is this possible?

96

A friend was telling me, "I have eight sons and each has one sister." In total, how many children does my friend have?

97

Ann's brother has one more brother than sisters. How many more brothers than sisters does Ann have?

98

"I have as many brothers as sisters, but my brothers have twice the number of sisters as brothers. How many of us are there?"

FAMILY TIES

99

A doctor has a brother who is an attorney in Alabama, but the attorney in Alabama does not have a brother who is a doctor. How can this be?

100

John wonders, "If Raymond's son is my son's father, how am I related to Raymond?"

101

If your uncle's sister is related to you, but is not your aunt, what is the relation?

102

A group of paleontologists found a prehistoric cave and one of them is congratulated by a younger son, who writes a telegram to his dad explaining the discovery. Who discovered the cave?

103

The other day, I heard the following conversation:

"Charles is related to you the same way I am to your son."

"And you are related to me in the same way Charles is to you."

How are Charles and the second man related?

104

Can someone marry his brother's wife's mother-in-law?

105

Ann is looking at the portrait of a gentleman. "He is not my father, but his mother was my mother's mother-in-law," she says. Who is this gentleman?

106

Do you know if the Catholic Church allows a man to marry his widow's sister?

107

A friend of mine was looking at a photo when she said, "Brothers and sisters? I have one. And this man's father is my father's son." Who was in the photo?

108

A friend of mine was looking at a photo when he said, "Brother and sisters? I have none. But this man's son is my father's son." Who was in the photo?

109

Two women are talking on the street. When they see two men coming, they say, "There are our fathers, our mothers' husbands, our children's fathers, and our own husbands." How can you explain this?

QUICK LOGIC

110

What was the biggest ocean in the world before Balboa discovered the Pacific Ocean?

111

How many cookies could you eat on an empty stomach?

112

Three mature and hefty women were walking in San Francisco under one regular-size umbrella. Why didn't they get wet?

113

What can a pitcher be filled with so it is lighter than when it is full of air?

114

A dog is tied to a 15-foot long leash. How can the dog reach a bone that is 20 feet away?

115

I went into a store and found out that it cost $3 for 400, which meant that each part cost $1. What did I want to buy?

116

Last week, my uncle Peter was able to turn his bedroom light off and get into bed before the room was dark. The light switch and the bed are ten feet apart. How did he accomplish this?

117

How can you make 30 cents with only two coins if one of the coins is not a nickel?

118

The only barber in my town likes foreigners to go into his shop. Last week, he was telling me, "The truth is that I'd rather give two foreigners haircuts than to give a haircut to one person in town." What was the logic behind this?

119

My brother Mark says he is able to place a bottle in the middle of a room and by crawling on the floor, he can slide into it. How can this be?

120

Last Friday I flew to San Diego. It was a scary flight. About an hour after getting onto the plane, I saw a very thick fog and then the engines stopped due to lack of fuel. Why didn't we die?

121

While eating out, my brother-in-law Paul found a fly in his coffee. After taking the cup away, the waiter came back with a different cup of coffee. My brother-in-law got upset and returned it, saying that the coffee in the second cup was the same as in the first one. How did he know?

122

You find shelter in a mountain lodge on a windy night. When you go in, you only find a match, a candle, a sheet of newspaper, and a torch. You need to light the fireplace. What would you light first?

123

A mother has six children and five potatoes. How can she feed each an equal amount of potatoes? (Do not use fractions.)

124

The giraffe and its offspring are walking in a field. The little giraffe tells a friend, "I am the daughter of this giraffe, although this giraffe is not my mother." How can you explain this?

125

A farmer has twenty sheep, ten pigs, and ten cows. If we call the pigs cows, how many cows will he have?

126

Where must a referee be to blow the whistle?

127

In the event of an emergency, can a Muslim baptize a Catholic?

128

It occurs once in a minute, twice in a week, and once in a year. What is it?

129

One night, when my uncle Emil was reading a book in the living room, his wife turned off the light and the living room became completely dark. However, my uncle continued reading. How is this possible?

130

A man says, "I am going to drink water because I don't have water. If I had it, I would drink wine." What does he do for a living?

131

Imagine you are a taxi driver and you are driving a 1978 yellow cab. Your passengers are an older couple, and they want to travel 6 miles. You are driving at 40 miles per hour with the tank one-third full, when, 2 miles into the trip, the tank is down to one-quarter full. Ten minutes later, the trip is over. What is the name and age of the cab driver?

132

A railway line has a double track, except in a tunnel where there was no room for a double track. A train goes into the tunnel in one direction, and another one enters in the opposite direction. Both trains are traveling fast. However, they do not crash. Why?

133

My son was telling me yesterday, "Four days ago, my school's soccer team won a game 4 to 1, although none of the boys on my school's team scored any goals. Also, the other team didn't score against itself accidentally." How can this be?

134

Last Thursday, my aunt Martha forgot her driver's license at home. She was traveling down a one way street in the wrong direction and did not stop at an intersection to let pedestrians go. A policeman was watching her, but did not give her a ticket. Why?

135

Three friends went out for drinks. The waiter brought them a check for $30, so each one of them paid $10. When the waiter took the cash, he realized he had made a mistake, and the check was for $25 instead. When he gave their change back, each friend got a dollar and they left the remaining two dollars as a tip. Therefore, each customer paid $9; multiplied by 3 this equals $27; plus $2 for the tip equals $29. Where is the remaining dollar?

136

A 16-year-old boy was driving a moped down a one-way street in the wrong direction. A policeman stopped him and gave him a ticket. The policeman paid the ticket himself. Can you find a logical explanation for this?

137

The butcher, his daughter, the fisherman, and his wife won the lottery and divided the prize into three. How can this be?

138

My friend Albert the butcher wears a size 13 shoe, is six feet tall, and wears a 42-long suit. What does he weigh?

139

There are five apples in one basket and five people in a room. How can you distribute the apples so that each person receives one and there is one apple left in the basket?

140

A man is doing his work. He knows that if his suit tears, he will die. Can you guess his job?

141

We have just invented two words: to sint and to sant. You cannot sint or sant in the street or in the office. You can do both things in the bathroom, the swimming pool, and the beach, but in the swimming pool and the beach you cannot sint completely. You cannot sint without clothes on and you need little or no clothing to sant. Can you guess what the words mean?

142

My cousin Henry can guess the score of a soccer game before the game begins. How can that be?

143

Before my husband left on a trip, he left me $150 in cash and a $500 check. However, when I went to the bank to cash the check, I found out that the account only had $450. How could I cash the check?

144

A bus stops three times during the ride. The ticket costs 12 cents to the first stop, 21 to the second stop, and 25 to the third stop. A man gets on at the start of the route and gives the driver 25 cents. Without talking to the passenger, the driver gives him a ticket to the last stop. How did the driver know?

145

You've probably heard the expression "two's company and three's a crowd." But what's the simplest way to describe four and five?

146

Mary, riding her white horse, decides to go into the forest. How far can she go?

147

What animal eats with its tail?

148

How can you light a match under water?

149

What three shapes can a saber have for it to fit in a sheath?

150

"This parrot can repeat anything it hears," the owner of the pet shop told Janice last week. So my sister bought it. Yesterday, she went to return it, claiming that the parrot had not even said one word. However, the pet shop owner had not lied to her. Can you explain this?

151

A man and his son were in a car accident. The boy had a fracture and injuries to one leg and was taken to a nearby hospital in an ambulance. When he was in the operating room, the surgeon said, "I cannot operate on him! He is my son!" Explain this.

152

Why do black sheep eat less grass than white sheep?

LOGIC

153

My cousin Mary dropped an earring in her coffee, but the earring did not get wet. How could this be?

154

I have a book where the foreword comes after the epilogue, the end is in the first half of the book, and the index comes before the introduction. What book is it?

155

How can you explain that one lady works alone as a bartender, yet there is a COUPLE that works behind the counter?

156

My uncle Raphael bought a coin in the flea market for 10 dollars. The coin has the head of Emperor Augustus and is dated 27 B.C. The other side is illegible. It is a fake, however. What proves that it is not a true ancient Roman coin?

157

An Air France plane crashes along the border of Portugal and Spain. Rescue teams from both countries are called to the site of the crash to help the victims. In which country do you think the survivors will be buried?

158

The director of a large company asks the security guard working the night shift to call him a cab, because he needs to take a red-eye flight to New York. The guard tells him not to board the plane, because he had just had a dream that the director would have an accident. To be safe, the director decides to wait until the next morning. During the trip, he reads in the paper that the red-eye flight had crashed. When he returns from his trip, he thanks the guard and gives him a bonus. Then he fires him. Why did he fire him?

159

My cousin Edward got soaked while he was walking on the street yesterday. He did not have an umbrella or a hat, so when he got home, his clothes were completely wet. However, not a hair on his head got wet. Why?

160

My sister Sophie lives on the 28th floor of a 32-story building. When my aunt Emily visits her, she takes the elevator to the 25th floor and then walks up the stairs. On her way down, she takes the elevator at the 28th floor all the way down to the ground floor. Why does she do this?

161

A man was sleeping in a hotel. In the middle of the night, he woke up and could not go back to sleep. He picked up the phone and called someone. As soon as he hung up, he fell sound asleep. He did not know the person he was calling. Why did he call that person?

162

When he goes to the bathroom, a man does not know if the hot water faucet is the one on the left or on the right. What does he need to do to be sure that he does not turn on the cold water before he turns on the hot water?

163

A man took his wife to the emergency room. The doctor decided to operate on her immediately. He told the husband that whether the wife died during the operation or survived, he would charge $1,000. The woman did not survive the operation. The husband did not pay anything. Why not?

164

The brothers Albert, Ben, Carl, and Don wear shirt sizes 37, 38, 39, and 40, respectively. Their mother bought one blue shirt for each one of them and embroidered their first initials on the left side. She placed three initials correctly. How many different ways can this happen?

165

If the date of the last Saturday of last month and the first Sunday of this month do not add up to 33, what month are we in?

166

The priest in my hometown announced last year that on a particular day he would walk on water for half an hour. The river was not dry and we could all see that the priest was actually able to walk on water. How did he manage?

167

Two miners go home after work. One of them has his face covered with soot and the other has a clean face. The one with a clean face wipes it with a handkerchief and the one with the dirty face does not do anything. Why?

168

What is there in the middle of a cigar?

169

A remote town has two hair salons. The first one has a dirty mirror, a floor covered with hair, and the hairdresser has an awful haircut. In the second one, the mirror and floor are very clean and the hairdresser has a great haircut. Where would you go and why?

170

A man ordered a glass of white wine and a glass of red wine at a bar. He took the glass of white wine in his right hand and the one with red in his left hand and drank both. He paid and left. The next day, he did the same. When he was leaving, the waiter asked him:

"I did not know that firemen drank that way."

The man smiled and left. How did the waiter know that he was a fireman?

171

Three meteorologists left a meeting in the middle of the night, during a heavy rain.

"The weather will remain like this until the next full moon," said one of them.

"I agree. And 96 hours from now, the sun will not shine," said the second one.

"I agree more with you than with the first forecast," said the third one.

Why was the third meteorologist so sure?

172

A criminal took his wife to the movies to watch a western. During a gunshot scene he killed his wife with a bullet to her heart. When he left the movies with his wife's dead body, nobody tried to stop him. How did he manage this?

173

In the 5th century A.D. a king was taking his daily bath when he received a huge crown that he had ordered made from one of his bars of gold. He knew that the crown and the gold weighed the same, although he suspected that part of the gold had been replaced with lighter materials, such as copper or silver. How did he find out quickly?

174

If I take two apples out of a basket containing six apples, how many apples do I have?

175

How much will a 38° angle measure when observed under a microscope that magnifies ten times?

176

John Peterson was born in Albany in 1938, on a date not divisible by 2, 3, or 5, and in a month that does not contain the letters "e" or "i." When does he become one year older?

177

A passenger traveling by bus between Springfield and Capital City noticed that due to the heavy traffic, it took him 80 minutes to reach his destination at an average speed of 40 mph. On his return trip, he took the bus and it took him 1 hour and 20 minutes at the same average speed and with less traffic. Do you know why?

178

A man traveling in a taxi is talking to the driver. After a while, the driver tells him, "You must excuse me, but I am deaf and cannot hear a word of what you are saying." The passenger stops talking. After he gets out of the cab, the passenger realizes that the driver had lied to him. How?

179

My friend told me the following story: "I was drinking a Coke in a bar when a man wearing a mustache came in and ordered a glass of water. As the waiter came back with his water, he pointed a gun at the customer. The customer got startled, but then calmed down and thanked the waiter." How can you explain what happened?

180

A 30-year-old man married a 25-year-old woman. She died at the age of 50 and her husband was so devastated that he cried for years. Ten years after he stopped crying, he died. However, he lived to be 80. How many years was he a widower?

181

Two rich men, now bankrupt, came across each other one day. After exchanging greetings and catching up with what had happened in their lives, they compared how much money each had. The first one had 80 dollars and the second one had only 42 dollars. However, two hours later, between both of them they had more than 84 million dollars in cash. None of them had inherited anything, won the lottery, or received payment for a debt or loan. How could this be?

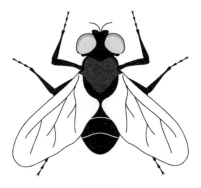

182

I am sitting at a table. Ten flies are on the table. With one swat, I kill three flies. How many flies are left on the table?

INTELLIGENCE AND SKILLS

183

How can you drop a matchbook match from five feet above the ground so that it comes to rest with one of its thin edges touching the ground?

184

How can you drop an egg a distance of three feet without breaking it?

185

How can you divide a round pie in eight equal pieces by cutting only three straight lines?

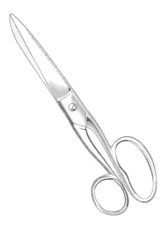

186

Two thin ropes hang from the high ceiling of an empty room, just too far apart from each other to be grabbed with both hands at the same time. How can you tie a knot with both rope ends using only a pair of sharp scissors?

187

A sparrow has fallen into a hole in a rock. The hole measures three inches in diameter and is three feet deep. Due to the depth of the hole, the sparrow cannot be reached by hand. We cannot use sticks or canes, because we could hurt the bird. How can you get the bird out?

188

A homeless man runs out of cigarettes. He looks for cigarette butts since he knows that he can make one new cigarette out of every three butts. He picks up nine butts. If he smokes one cigarette per hour, how many hours can he smoke for?

189

How can you make a hole in a paper napkin and then fit your body through it without tearing the napkin?

190

How can you form four equilateral triangles with six toothpicks of equal length?

191

You go on a picnic with your friends. Each one of them wants a different amount of oil and vinegar in his salad. However, you've already mixed the oil and vinegar in one bottle. How can you please everyone at the picnic?

192

The maximum length of a postal package is 30 inches. How can you mail an iron bar that measures 40 inches in length without bending it?

193

How can you tie a knot with a napkin by holding one end in each hand without letting go of it?

194

If you cut a circle the size of a nickel in a piece of paper, can you pass a silver dollar through it?

195

A six-foot long rope is tied to a hook fixed to the ceiling of a room. We tie a mug by the handle to the loose end of the rope. If you cut the rope in half, how can you prevent the mug from falling? (There is nothing between the floor and the mug. Nobody is holding on to the mug.)

196

Two thick ropes hang from a high ceiling attached to hooks three feet apart. The ends touch the ground. Without using anything else, and considering that you will die if you fall from one-quarter of the height of the room, how can you cut the largest amount possible of each rope with a knife?

197

You are playing table tennis on the beach when your only ball falls into a hole in the sand that someone else had used for their beach umbrella. The hole is only slightly larger in diameter than the ball. How can you take the ball out without digging?

198

A truck is about to go under a bridge, although its load is two inches higher than the clearance of the bridge. It is a very heavy load, so it cannot be unloaded. How can it pass under the bridge in a quick and simple way?

199

How could you throw a tennis ball so that after traveling a short distance, it stops and returns following the same path? The ball cannot hit or be tied to anything.

200

A brick measuring 5 centimeters high, 20 centimeters long, and 10 centimeters wide falls off a dike causing a leak that must be stopped immediately. How can you stop the leak with a saw and a wooden cylinder measuring 5 centimeters in diameter?

201

With your pants on, can you put your right hand in your left pocket and your left hand in your right pocket?

202

I bet that you alone cannot take off your left shoe using only your right hand. I will not touch you or interfere with your movements. How can I prevent this?

203

How can you pour wine out of a corked bottle that is half full without breaking or damaging the bottle or the cork, and without taking out the cork?

204

You keep some of your diamonds in a jewelry case with a sliding cover. To keep thieves away, you put a scorpion inside the case. One day you need to take some of the diamonds. How can you do it without taking the scorpion out, while protecting your hands from its bites, only taking a few seconds, and leaving the case in the same way you originally had it?

205

I am going to make you a bet: "On this folded piece of paper I have written down the prediction of something that might or might not happen in the next five minutes. Put it in your pocket. On this blank piece of paper, write "YES" if you think that it will happen and "NO" if you think it will not happen. I'll bet you a cup of coffee that you cannot guess right." What have I written on the paper? (It is something that can be proven.)

206

Your rich relative gathers the family together to tell them, "I will leave my inheritance to the one who can collect the exact number of pennies equaling half the number of days that I have left to live." What would you do to inherit the fortune?

207

How can two people step on one page of newspaper so that they can't touch each other without stepping off the newspaper?

208

A friend told me, "I can do something that you are not able to, no matter how hard you try." What could it be?

209

A bottle is standing on a rug (or upside down on a dollar bill). Can you take out the rug or the bill without turning or touching the bottle and without help from anybody else?

210

Set an imaginary finish line somewhere (for example, a point on the wall 10 feet away from you). Find a method of advancing so that even though you always move ahead, you never reach the finish line.

211

Yesterday, someone dared me to jump over a ballpoint pen on the floor. I could not, even though I'm a good jumper. How come I wasn't able to?

INVESTIGATIONS AND TRIALS

212

A plane was hijacked. The hijacker demanded two parachutes and ten million dollars. Once he got both, he jumped off the plane during the night and while in flight. Why did he need two parachutes?

213

One rainy day, my cousin Ernest found a dead body lying next to a strange package. He could not see any footprints in the area. Because of the temperature of the body, Ernest knew that the man had been dead for less than one hour. What was in the package? How did the man get there?

214

A man walking along a rural road was being sought by the police. When he saw a patrol car approaching him, he thought of running toward the forest. Instead, he ran 20 yards toward the approaching car. Why?

215

Stella was telling my cousin Ernest that her husband once fell asleep in the opera and started dreaming of being on a plane that was hijacked. The hijacker demanded to fly to an African country. People complained, screamed, and fainted. The hijacker was pointing a gun to Stella's husband's head. At this point, the husband started to move and make noise. Stella tapped her husband on the shoulder and he got so startled that he fell on the floor and died from the impact. Ernest immediately said, "This story is impossible." How did he know?

Quick-to-Solve Brainteasers

216

My cousin Ernest solved this case. A man was hanged, his feet half a meter above the ground, in the middle of a very hot room, hanging by a rope tied to a hook from the ceiling. The room was completely empty and had some moisture on the floor. On the other side of the door there was a ladder, which must have been used by the victim. However, the investigation proved that the victim had no place to lean the ladder against to reach the rope. That is how Ernest realized that this was not a murder, but a suicide. How could it have happened?

217

Last winter, my cousin Ernest went on a ski vacation. At the airport, he read in the papers that a famous couple had been skiing and the wife had died in an accident. Her well-known husband was the only eyewitness. After talking to a travel agent, my cousin was able to deduce that it had not been an accident. What did he find out from the travel agent?

218

A medieval count organized a court trial in which he gave the defendant a chance to save his life if he could pick a white marble out of a bag containing, in the count's words, one white marble and one black marble. The accused knew that this was a trick, because he had seen the count place two black marbles in the bag. However, he went ahead and took out a marble. What did he do to save his life?

219

During the war, my cousin Ernest was captured and put into a prison cell. It was in the basement, with a dirt floor, armored walls, and a water tank 10 feet from the ground. There was no furniture and no object to reach the water tank with. How did Ernest manage to drink?

220

My cousin Ernest, amateur private investigator, was able to figure out the weapon used in a suicide case. The man had been stabbed, but the weapon was nowhere in the room. The room was locked from the inside. The deceased had the only key. During the investigation, they found out that the weapon had been thicker than typical knives. What was the weapon? Where was it?

221

When Ernest went to visit his friend Albert, he found him dead on his desk with a bullet through the head. He saw a cassette player and decided to listen to the tape. He hit play and heard, "This is Albert. I just got a call saying that someone is on his way here to kill me and that he will be here in less than three minutes. I hear steps. Someone is opening the door." At that point, my cousin knew that it was not Albert's voice on the tape, but the killer's. How did he know that?

222

A man has been killed in a room locked from the inside with a vertical deadbolt. The killer was able to lock it from the outside. How did he do this?

Quick-to-Solve Brainteasers

223

A businessman was working in his home office when he realized he had left a five-dollar bill in the book he had been reading. He called his butler to bring him the book from the library. When he got the book, the bill was no longer there. He then questioned the maid and the butler. The maid remembered seeing the bill between pages 99 and 100 in a book to the left of a business book. The butler did not recall seeing the bill, but was sure the book was to the right of the business book, because to the left of it there was a statistics book.

Who is lying?

224

On the 29th of last month, there was a double murder on the express train from Paris to Berlin. The driver and the conductor were killed at the same time, even though they were at opposite ends of the train. This was confirmed by a police detective, who was at the exact center of the train and heard both gunshots at the same time.

When my cousin was told this story, he realized that both victims did not die at the same time.

How did he figure it out?

225

Two people were accused of murder. In a court trial, one had been acquitted and the other had been found guilty. When the judge had to sentence the guilty man, he said, "This is the strangest case that I have ever presided over. Even though you have been found guilty, the law obliges me to set you free." Can you explain this?

226

My cousin Ernest was once kidnapped. He knew they would either take him to New York City or to Sydney, Australia. When they took his blindfold off, he could see he had been locked in a room without windows. There was only a table, a bed, a chair, and a sink. However, Ernest was able to figure out which city he was in. How did he do it?

227

These are the clues to a robbery and murder on a ground floor office:

A. The killer had to be one of these three people: the muscly engineer, the obese director, or the perky secretary.

B. The stolen goods were taken out from the open window. There were light footprints under it in the snow.

C. The footprints matched the director's shoes, which were found next to the crime weapon.

D. Only one bullet was found, although there were two wounds to the body, one to the chest and the other to the right hand.

Who was the killer? Why were there two wounds?

RIDDLES

228

I climbed up a cherry tree, where I found cherries. I did not pick cherries, nor did I leave cherries. How can you explain this?

229

What animal walks on all fours in the morning, on two legs at noon, and on three legs at dusk?

230

What is so fragile that when you say its name you break it?

231

Among my siblings I am the thinnest. I am in Paris, but I am not in France. Who am I?

232

I can only live when there is light, although I die if the light shines on me. What am I?

ELEMENTS IN MOVEMENT

233

A ship is anchored offshore. In order for the crew to reach the rafts, they must descend a 22-step ladder. Each step is 10 inches high. The tide rises at a ratio of 5 inches per hour. How many steps will the tide have covered after 10 hours?

234

A 100-meter long train moving 100 meters per minute must pass through a tunnel of 100 meters in length. How long will it take?

Quick-to-Solve Brainteasers

235

A train headed for Barcelona leaves Madrid at midnight, at a constant speed of 60 kilometers per hour. Another train leaves Barcelona at the same time, heading for Madrid at a constant speed of 40 kilometers per hour. The distance between both cities is 600 kilometers. The train that left from Madrid stops for half an hour when both trains cross. Which train was closer to Madrid when they crossed?

236

My uncle Lou takes the subway to the movies or the theater every evening. He always takes the first subway that stops at the station close to his home, no matter which direction it is heading. If the subway is heading north, he will go to the theater. If it is heading south, he will go to the movies. Both trains run every 10 minutes. However, nine times out of every ten, my uncle ends up at the movies. How can you explain this?

237

A cyclist takes 2 minutes and 13 seconds for every full lap of a circuit. Answer in 10 seconds: How long will he take to do 60 laps?

238

My bird can fly faster than any supersonic plane. How can this be?

239

Albert, who was just back from his trip around the world in a sailboat, asked me, "What part of my boat has traveled the longest distance?"

Do you know the answer to that?

240

If we tie a light oxygen tank to a bird so that it can breathe on the moon, would the bird fly faster, slower, or the same speed as it does on earth? (Remember that there is less gravity on the moon.)

241

What can a train passenger do to be in a tunnel the least time possible while the train is going through a 100-meter long tunnel?

242

Two trains travel on parallel tracks in opposite directions, at 70 and 50 miles per hour. When the trains are 60 miles apart, a bird flying at 80 miles per hour leaves the first train and flies off to the second. It keeps on flying back and forth until both trains cross. How many miles does the bird fly?

243

We drag a large stone over three logs measuring 50 inches in circumference each. What distance does the stone cover each time the logs make one rotation?

244

Two trains are moving on the same track in opposite directions. One goes 80 meters per minute and the other 120 meters per minute. After 12 hours, they are 1700 meters apart. How far apart will they be one minute before they collide?

245

A snail is climbing up a one-meter high wall. It advances three centimeters per minute and then stops for one minute to rest, during which it slides back down two centimeters. How long will the snail take to reach the top of the wall?

246

A young man gets on the end car of a train. Just as the train passes by Cat City, he leaves his suitcases and walks at a steady pace to find a seat. After five minutes, he reaches the front car. Not finding a seat, he returns at the same pace to where his luggage is. At that point, the train passes by Dog City, which is five miles from Cat City. How fast is the train going?

247

A journey by ship between New York and London takes seven days. Ships leave from both ports at the same time every day. During a trip, how many other ships will a ship come across?

248

A regular LP record measures 30 centimeters in diameter. The outer blank (non-recorded) area is 5 millimeters in width. The non-playable center area measures 10 centimeters in diameter. The grooves are ¼ millimeter apart. What is the distance traveled by the needle during the time that the record is playing?

249

A man is walking at night at a steady pace. As he passes by a street lamp, he notices that his shadow becomes longer. Does the top of the shadow move faster, slower, or the same when the shadow is longer as when it is shorter?

250

A kid who is in the back seat of a car is holding the string of a helium balloon. The balloon is floating without touching the roof of the car, and the windows are closed. When the car accelerates, where does the balloon go? And when the car turns, where does it go?

251

A train goes from north to south, although at all times there are certain areas of the train that are moving in a south-to-north direction. What are these areas?

252

A railway track measures 5 kilometers in length and its ties are one meter apart. A child ties a can to a dog's tail. As the dog starts running along the tracks, it increases its speed by one meter per second every time it hears the noise of the can hitting a tie. If the dog starts to run at a speed of 1 meter/second and the can hits all of the railway ties, what is the dog's speed at the end of the track?

253

Two athletes ran in a 100-meter race. When the runner with the number "1" on his jersey reached the finish line, the runner with number "2" had only run 95 meters. In a second race, the number "1" runner had to start 5 meters behind the start line. If both ran at the same speed as in the first race, who won this time?

254

A driver always leaves the office at the same time, gets to the director's house at the same time, picks him up, and takes him to the office. One morning, the director decides to leave one hour earlier and he starts walking to the office along his usual route. When he sees the car, he gets in and continues his trip. He reaches the office 20 minutes earlier than usual. How long was he walking for?

255

In a river without a current, a ship leaves from a certain point, goes three miles up the river, turns around and goes back to the point of departure in 20 minutes. If the river has a current of two miles per hour and the ship did the same trip at the same speed (with respect to the water), would the trip last more or less than 20 minutes?

Quick-to-Solve Brainteasers

256

A mountaineer starts rapidly climbing up a mountain trail at 6 A.M. He makes frequent and irregular stops to rest or eat. He reaches the summit at 6 P.M. At 6 A.M. the next day, he starts his way back following the same route, stopping only once to eat. He reaches the starting point at 6 P.M. Is there a point on the way where he passes at exactly the same time on both days?

OUTDOORS

257

Which is warmer, a two-inch thick blanket or two blankets one inch thick each?

258

Three ice cubes are melting in a glass of water. Once they have completely melted, has the water level of the glass changed?

259

A super-accurate bomb, one that always hits the bull's-eye and destroys it, hits an indestructible fort. What will happen?

260

A man gets up 180 times every night and sleeps for at least 7 hours at a stretch. Where does he live?

261

I had just made myself a cup of coffee when I realized I had to run upstairs for a moment. I did not want the coffee to get cold, and I had to add milk at room temperature. Should I add the milk before I go up or after I get back?

262

A raft loaded with rocks is floating in a swimming pool. We mark the level of water in the swimming pool and on the raft. If we drop the rocks into the pool, what will happen to the water level in the pool and to the flotation line of the raft? Will they go up or down?

263

A boat is floating in a pool. We mark the flotation line. If we drop rocks into the pool and make the water level rise five inches, will the water rise more or less than five inches compared to the mark we made on the boat?

264

Two ivy branches sprout out of a tree trunk from the same point at ground level. One wraps around four times to the right, the other wraps around five times to the left, and their ends meet. Without counting the ends, how many times do both branches of ivy intersect?

265

An African trader is visiting different tribes in a raft loaded with sacks of salt, which he trades according to their weight in gold.

When he is about to trade them, he realizes that the scale is broken. How can he trade the same weight of salt for gold?

A LITTLE BIT OF EVERYTHING

266

We have a bottle of wine approximately three-fourths full. We want to leave an amount of wine in the bottle equal to exactly half of the total capacity of the bottle. How can we do it without using anything to help us?

267

We have three glass pitchers. One is a three-quart pitcher and is empty. The twelve-quart one is also empty. The third one is clear in color and irregular in shape. It contains acid. It has two marks, a two-quart mark and a five-quart mark. The level of acid is a little less than five quarts. We want to take out exactly three quarts of acid, but when we try it, the three-quart pitcher breaks. What can we do to take out the desired amount by pouring it into the twelve-quart pitcher, which is the only one left?

268

A man was used to walking at a regular pace. He never wore a watch, although he had a very accurate clock at home. One day, he forgot to wind it and the clock stopped. He went to a friend's house two miles from his home to ask the time. He spent the afternoon with him and when he came back home, he set the clock to the exact time. How did he know the exact time?

269

We have two similar coins and we make one spin on the edge of the other. How many times does the spinning coin turn on itself each time it makes an entire lap around the stationary one?

270

Mr. Brown, Mr. White, and Mr. Red are in a meeting. The three are wearing ties that are the three colors of their last names, although no man's tie matches his name. Mr. Brown asks the man with the white tie if he likes red, but cannot hear the answer. What is the color of each man's tie?

271

We mark three random points on a sphere. How likely are the three points to be in the same hemisphere?

Quick-to-Solve Brainteasers

272

Can you draw a square with two straight lines?

LAUGHS

273

My cousin Henry can predict the future when he pets his black poodle. Is that possible?

274

An older woman and her young daughter, a young man, and an older man are traveling in the same compartment of a train. When the train passes through a tunnel, they hear a kiss and a slap. As the lights come back on, they can see the older man with a black eye. This is what each of the passengers thought:

The older woman: "He deserved it. I am glad my daughter can defend herself."

The daughter: "I cannot believe he preferred to kiss my mother or that young man over kissing me."

The older man: "What is going on here? I didn't do anything! Maybe the young man tried to kiss the girl, and she mistakenly slapped me."

The young man: "I know what really happened."

Do you know what happened?

275

An electric train runs at 60 mph heading south toward a wind blowing at 30 mph. What is the direction of the smoke from the train?

276

If Albert's peacock jumps over the fence onto Edward's property and lays an egg there, whose egg is it?

277

What can you have in an empty pocket? (Apart from air, of course.)

278

What did the twelve apostles make?

279

My cousin Herbert told me yesterday, "I can easily bite my eye." How can this be?

280

It sings and has ten feet. What is it?

Quick-to-Solve Brainteasers

281

Mary married John two years ago. She did not bring any money into the marriage and did not work during these two years, but she made her husband a millionaire. How did she do it?

282

My cousin Herbert told me this morning, "I can easily bite my good eye." How can he do this?

283

What can elephants make that no other animal can?

284

Last Thursday I walked back home from work (2 miles), and noticed a strange man following me the entire way. Once I got home, the man was still there walking around my building (a 100-by-100-yard square building). Later on, I saw he had fallen asleep next to the street lamp at the entrance of my building. During which lap did he fall asleep?

285

How can you get into your home if there is a dangerous dog inside that doesn't know you and belongs to your wife's friend?

286

A turtle, a gopher, and a hare are walking one behind the other in a straight line.

"I am first," said the turtle.

"I am second," said the gopher.

"I am first," said the hare.

How can you explain these statements?

287

What activity can only be done at night?

288

My cousin Robert was pushed into a well measuring six feet in diameter and 10 feet deep, with smooth walls and its bottom covered with water. How did he emerge from the well?

289

Every day, a cyclist crosses the border between Spain and France carrying a bag. No matter how much customs officials investigate him, they do not know what he is smuggling. Do you?

ANSWERS

1. Only once, because the second time you will be subtracting from 24 instead of 30.

2. The number 8. (It is made up of two zeroes, one on top of the other.)

3. By using Roman numerals. The upper half of XII is VII.

4. 1 and 9.

5. Any number and 1.

6. 2 and 2.

7. It is easy to eliminate possibilities. For example, it has to be an even number; none of the digits can be zero (or else the product would be zero); and the product of the digits must be less than or equal to 48 (otherwise two times the product would have three digits). If you think of the remaining possibilities, you will find the answer, $36 = 2 \times 3 \times 6$.

8. 1, 2, and 3, because $1 \times 2 \times 3 = 1 + 2 + 3 = 6$.

9. $25 = 5^2$ and $36 = 6^2$.

10. $9^{9^9} = 9^{387420489}$, which is a number with more than 369 million digits.

11. The father is 41 and the son is 14.

12. 10 cents.

13. $1.10 for the outlet and $0.10 for the light bulb.

14. $3 \times 75 = 225$ qualities distributed among 100 persons, so at least 25% of them have all three.

15. The number of passing grades is a whole number less than 32, and 5% of it is also a whole number. It can only be 20. If 20 is the number of passing grades, the number of students from New York that took the test is one.

16. If half of the 83% tip the usher 10 cents and the other half doesn't, it is the same as if all 83% had tipped him 5 cents, which is the same amount as what the remaining 17% tipped. The usher received 4,800 cents, or more simply, 48 dollars.

17. Turn the page upside-down. It will read $108 = 6 \times 18$.

18. He will need twenty "9's," one for the numbers 9, 19, 29, 39, 49, 59, 69, 79, 89, 90, 91, 92, 93, 94, 95, 96, 97, and 98, and two for 99.

19. At each stop, passengers can buy a ticket for any of the 24 remaining stops. Therefore, the number of tickets will be $25 \times 24 = 600$.

20. Let's imagine that the inhabitants are as different as possible (one will be bald, another will have only one hair, another two, another three, and so on, until we get to someone having 100,000 hairs). Inhabitant number 100,002 will have the same number of hairs as someone among the first 100,001 inhabitants. The total population is more than 200,000 people, which means that there will be more than 100,000 inhabitants with the same number of hairs as other people in town.

21. Three: one red, one blue, and one brown.

22. There are 6 chestnut trees per side, making a total of 12.

23. Two birds and one olive tree.

24. There is only one winner, so the remaining 110 players were defeated in 110 matches. Therefore, they used 110 balls.

25. Twelve muffins. When John ate half the remaining muffins plus three more to leave none, he must have eaten six muffins. So Peter ate half the muffins and left six, meaning that there were twelve to start.

26. The shepherd that is talking had 5 sheep and the other one had 7.

27. Three cages and four canaries.

28. Each sardine costs 1 dollar. Therefore, 7½ sardines would cost 7½ dollars.

29. Since ½ brick weighs 3 pounds, 1½ bricks weigh 9 pounds.

30. Since 18 sardines is the same as 1½ dozen, they cost 9½ dollars.

31. Since 1 man eats 1 pie in 1½ minutes, 1 man eats 20 pies in 30 minutes, which means 3 men eat 60 pies in 30 minutes.

32. 11 times (one fewer than the number of times he went in).

33. Three ducks.

34. The person who won three games must have also lost six games, since his opponent won $3. In total, they played 9 games.

35. We measure the inside diameter and the height of the liquid, obtaining the volume of the liquid. Then, we turn the bottle upside-down and measure the volume of the empty part. If we add both, we obtain the total capacity of the bottle and can calculate the percentage of the liquid. An easier way is to measure only both heights, because both have the same size base.

36. $0.0125

37. By leaving a task half done (for example, peeling potatoes) so that the next soldier can finish it, they can do all the tasks in 1 hour and 30 minutes.

38. 29 days. One spider would have covered half of the space on the 29th day, and on the 30th day would repeat what had been done, covering the space completely. Two spiders would each have covered half of the space in 29 days, therefore covering the entire area.

39. At 8 P.M. Each hour the volume triples, so it is one-third full one hour before it is full.

40. If the length of the rope + 2 yards = 3 times the length of the rope, then the rope is 1 yard long.

41. If the length is 6 yards + half the length, then half the length is 6 yards. Therefore, it is 12 yards long.

42. No mud at all, because a hole can only contain air.

43. There are only three people, a daughter, her mother, and her grandmother. The mother received 25 books from the grandmother and then gave 8 to her daughter.

44. Dolores is taller than Emily, who is taller than Ann.

45. Joan is 6 years older than Rose.

46. Emily speaks in a softer voice than Dolores (Emily < Ann < Dolores).

47. Peter is sitting between Philip (on his right) and James (on his left).

48. A pound of $10 gold coins has twice the amount of gold than half a pound of $20 coins. Therefore, it is worth more.

49. The store lost $40 given as change plus the value of the umbrella, $10. The transaction was only between the sales person and the customer. The bank teller did not take part in the transaction.

50. The pitcher with water contains exactly the same amount of wine as water in the pitcher of wine. Both pitchers have the same volume of liquid before and after mixing water and wine, so mixing them makes no difference.

51. He made each candidate ride another candidate's horse. Each one would, of course, try to come in first, because in that way the owner of the horse that a particular candidate was riding would lose the race.

52. The weight of the fish bowl increases by the same amount as the weight of the liquid displaced by the fish.

53. If it is a traditional scale with two dishes, you can place the apples in one dish and dirt in the other until they balance. Then, replace the apples with weights and you will know the weight of the apples. If it is a spring scale, you weigh the apples first, then write down the mark on the scale and replace the apples with weights until you reach the previous mark. The weights will show the real weight of the apples.

54. The reaction of the air that the little bird is pushing down in order to fly will partially affect both the dish of the scale and the floor of the room. The scale will show one pound minus some portion of the 5 ounces that the bird weighs.

   If the cage were sealed, the air would affect only the dish of the scale and the scale would continue to read one pound.

55. One weighing. Take one ball from the first sack, two from the second, three from the third, and so on until you reach the last sack, from which you take ten balls. Since $1 + 2 + 3 + ... + 9 + 10 = 55$, if all of the balls weighed 10 ounces each, the total weight would be 550 ounces. In this case, the weight will be $550 - N$, where N is the number of the sack containing nine-ounce balls.

56. We identify each sack by the number of balls taken from it. We must find a way to obtain different results from all possible sums of the digits that identify the sacks. The easiest way would be powers of 2: 1, 2, 4, 8, 16, ... (2^0, 2^1, 2^2, 2^3, 2^4, ...). Therefore, we will take one ball from one sack, two from another, four from another, etc.

The resulting weight will be 1023 – N, where N can only be obtained by adding certain sack numbers. If N is 27 ounces, the sacks containing 9-ounce balls will be those from which we took 1, 2, 8, and 16 balls, because, using just the powers of 2, 27 can only be obtained by adding 1 + 2 + 8 + 16.

Let's call "1" the sack from which we took 1 ball, "2" the one from which we took 2 balls, "3" the one from which we took 4 balls, etc. The number 27, in binary, is 11011. The position of the 1's in this binary sequence reveals the solution. The 1's are in first, second, fourth, and fifth position, which means that the sacks containing the 9-ounce balls are 1, 2, 4, and 5.

57. The best solution is to open four links from one of the pieces and use them to join the remaining five parts in one chain. The total cost will be 4 × 60 = 240 cents, or $2.40.

58. By cutting the third link, we obtain three pieces of one, two, and four links each. The first day, she pays with the one-link part. The second day, she pays with the two-link part and gets the one-link piece back as change. The third day, she pays with the loose link. The fourth day, she pays with the four-link part and receives back the three links, and so on.

59. The minimum number of parts that could have been left is 3 (the link that is cut and the two disconnected parts of the chain). The maximum number will be 6, as shown in the figure below.

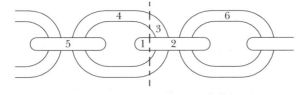

60. Two glasses. Pick up the second glass, pour its contents into the ninth glass, and put it back. Then pick up the fourth glass, pour its contents into the seventh glass, and put it back. Note that the seventh and ninth glasses are not moved.

61. 100% probability, because if four marbles are in their corresponding cups, the fifth one must be in its corresponding cup, too.

62. Three. The first two can be of different colors, white and black, but the third sock will be one of these two colors, and thus complete one pair.

63. Four. There are three different colors, so the first three socks may not match, but the fourth one will match one of the previous three socks.

64. 13. The first 12 gloves can be six white left gloves and six black left gloves. Therefore, the 13th glove will make a pair with one of the previous 12 gloves. No matter what the first 12 gloves are, if no two have made a pair yet, the 13th will.

65. 6. The worst case is to take two white, two black, and the red marble. The sixth marble has to be either white or black.

66. Put five marbles in one cup, four in another, and one in another. Put the cup with one marble inside the one containing four. There are other solutions, all based on the same trick. Another solution, for example, involves putting three marbles in one cup, three marbles in the second cup, and four marbles in the third cup, and then putting the second cup inside the third one. This leaves three marbles in the first cup, three marbles in the second cup, and seven marbles in the third cup.

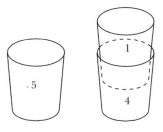

67. Put one marble in one box, three in another and five in a third one. Then place the three boxes inside the fourth box.

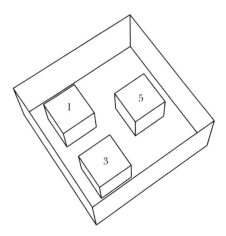

68. Take one marble from the box marked BW. If it is white, the other marble must also be white. This means that the box marked BB must have black and white marbles and the box marked WW must have only black marbles. You can apply the same principle if the first marble you take is black.

69. After being inverted twice, the hourglass continued working in its initial position. Therefore, the extra hour that it measured was a consequence of these two inversions, half an hour each time. If it was inverted for the second time at 11:30, the first time had to be a half-hour earlier, at 11:00.

70. The clock that doesn't work will show the precise time twice a day, but the fast one will take $2 \times 60 \times 12 = 1440$ days to show the precise time. Therefore, the broken clock shows the correct time more often.

71. Time to have the clock fixed.

72. Ten times (you can verify it yourself).

73. Four seconds (it takes two seconds between 2 consecutive strikes).

74. Four hours, the time between 8 and 12.

75. There is 1 second between 2 strikes. Therefore, it will take 11 seconds for the clock to strike 12 times.

76. He lived 59 years, because there is no "0" year.

77. He would have drunk the same number of cups of coffee. The difference is that the conversation would have taken place on March 14.

78. Friday.

79. Three days and two nights. She left yesterday and will return tomorrow.

80. The man's birthday is December 31 and he was talking on January 1. He's 36 now, the day before yesterday he was 35, this calendar year he will turn 37, and next calendar year he will turn 38.

81. It happened to Gioacchino Rossini, who was born on February 29, 1792, and who died on November 13, 1868. Remember that 1800 was not a leap year. All years that are divisible by four are leap years, except those that end in "00." They are only leap years if they are divisible by 400.

82. INVENT.

83. Neither. The yolk of an egg is yellow.

84. It is not "I am going in" or "I am not going in." The opposite is "I am leaving."

85. The word "incorrectly."

86. Lounger.

87. It's a matter of language. Consider "four twenty" as $4.20. Then it is true.

88. Yes. "Paris" starts with a "p," and "ends" starts with an "e."

89. The phone operator was trying to get the spelling of the man's last name. Therefore it makes no sense to ask, "I as in what?" The operator had already understood it was an "I."

90. The letter "i."

91. Let's suppose it is false. By saying "This statement is false," it becomes true and vice versa. Therefore, to be false it has to be true and vice versa. It is a paradox.

92. The letter "u."

93. He will not change his mind.

94. His statement must be "I will be hanged." If they want to hang him, the sentence is true, and therefore, they will not be able to hang him. For the same reason, he cannot be drowned because his statement would be false and they could not drown him if his statement is false. (Based on *Don Quixote*, by Cervantes.)

95. Yes, as long as the other half are male, too. She has five sons.

96. Nine children.

97. Three more brothers than sisters. Ann's brother has one more brother than sister. Ann is one of the sisters, so Ann will have one fewer sister than her brother has and one more brother than her brother has.

98. Seven. The only possible solution is that the person talking is a woman and there are four women and three men.

99. The doctor is a woman.

100. John is Raymond's son.

101. Your mother.

102. The son's mother.

103. The second man is Charles's grandson.

104. No, because it would be his mother.

105. The man is Ann's uncle.

106. If the man left a widow, then he is dead. Therefore, he cannot get married.

107. She was looking at a photo of her nephew.

108. He was looking at a photo of his father.

109. Two widowers have one daughter each and decide to marry each other's daughters. This conversation takes place once they are married and with children. Their wives are the ones talking.

110. The Pacific Ocean. Even though it had not been discovered or named by Balboa, it was still the biggest ocean.

111. One cookie, because after eating one you would no longer have an empty stomach.

112. Because it wasn't raining.

113. Holes.

114. By walking and dragging the rope with it. The puzzle does not say that the leash is tied to something.

115. The number 400, to hang on a house. This number is formed by three digits, at $1 each.

116. It was daytime, so the room was light.

117. With one quarter and one nickel. The puzzle says that one of the coins is not a nickel, and it is true since a quarter is not a nickel.

118. Because he earns double by giving a haircut to two foreigners instead of to only one person in town.

119. He goes to the next room and by crawling toward the bottle, he slides into the room.

120. The plane had not yet taken off.

121. He had already put sugar in his coffee.

122. The match.

123. By serving mashed potatoes.

124. It is a male giraffe, so it is the father and not the mother of the offspring.

125. Ten cows. We can call the pigs cows, but it doesn't make them cows.

126. He must always be behind the whistle.

127. There is no reason to baptize him. If he is Catholic, he is already baptized.

128. The letter "e."

129. My uncle Emil is blind, and he was reading in Braille.

130. He is a farmer. He needs plenty of water, so if he lacks water he has no income and he won't be able to buy or even make wine.

131. At the beginning of the puzzle, it says that you are the cab driver. Therefore, the answer is your name and age.

132. One of the trains went into the tunnel hours after the other.

133. It was a girls' team.

134. My aunt Martha was a pedestrian, too.

135. The customers paid $27, $25 to cover their bill and $2 as a tip for the waiter.

136. The driver of the moped was the policeman's son.

137. The butcher's daughter is the fisherman's wife.

138. Since he's a butcher, he weighs meat.

Quick-to-Solve Brainteasers

139. The first four people pick one apple each, and the fifth one takes the basket with the apple in it.

140. Either a deep-sea diver or an astronaut.

141. "To sint" means to take off your clothes, and "to sant" is to go into the water to bathe.

142. Because before the game begins, the score is always 0-0.

143. I deposited $50 in my bank account to have enough funds to cash the check.

144. The passenger gave the driver 25 cents in the form of four nickels and five pennies.

145. Nine.

146. As far as half of the forest, because if she went any further, she would be leaving the forest, instead of going into it.

147. All the animals that have one, because as far as we know, no animal takes it off to eat.

148. You just have to light a match under a container with water.

149. Straight, arced, or spiral.

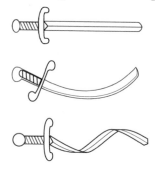

150. The parrot was deaf.

151. The surgeon was the boy's mother.

152. Because there are fewer black sheep than white sheep.

153. She dropped her earring into her coffee beans.

154. The dictionary. The word "foreword" comes before "epilogue," "end" is in the first half of the dictionary, and "index" comes before "introduction."

155. The girl's name is Anne COUPLE.

156. If it were an authentic coin, it could not have "B.C." (This system was created after Jesus died, not before he was born.)

157. Neither country, because they are survivors.

158. What the director actually needed was a real night shift guard that did not sleep at work, even if he could predict the future in his dreams.

159. My cousin Edward is bald. Therefore, his hair cannot get wet.

160. My aunt is really short and the button for the 25th floor is at the highest point she can reach.

161. The neighbor was snoring. That is why he couldn't sleep. When he made the call, the person woke up and stopped making noise.

162. He must turn on both faucets at the same time.

163. The woman died before the operation.

164. If three of the letters are correct, the fourth one must be too. Therefore, there is only one way.

165. The same month you are reading this.

166. The river was frozen.

167. When he sees his coworker, the miner with the clean face assumes that his face is also dirty and wipes it. The miner with a dirty face sees his coworker with a clean face and assumes that his is also clean.

168. The letter "g."

169. Hairdressers don't cut their own hair. Therefore, the clean hairdresser gave the bad haircut and the dirty hairdresser gave the perfect haircut. Thus, it is better to go to the dirty salon.

170. The customer was in his firefighter uniform.

171. Because in 96 hours it would again be night.

172. It was a drive-in theater. He killed her in the car. On his way out, nobody noticed that the woman was dead in the car.

173. First he immersed the crown in a container of water and measured the level of the water. Then he removed the crown and immersed the gold bar, measuring the water level. If the levels were not the same, the gold had been mixed with another metal.

174. Two apples.

175. It will still be 38°.

176. On his birthday.

177. He took the same time in both cases, because 1 hour and 20 minutes equals 80 minutes.

178. If the cab driver had been deaf, he would not have heard the address the passenger had given to him. He only mentioned he was deaf when the passenger didn't stop talking.

179. The waiter scared his customer who had the hiccups. That is why the customer thanked the waiter.

180. If he became a widower when he was 55 and died when he was 80, he was a widower for 25 years.

181. One was standing at the main door of a bank and his friend was standing at the back door. There was 84 million dollars in the safe of the bank. Therefore, "between both of them" they had that amount of money.

182. I killed three flies. They remain. The rest would have flown away immediately.

183. By bending the match and then dropping it.

184. Drop it and catch it before it hits the ground.

185. Cutting it either of these ways:

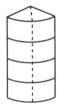

186. Tie the scissors to one of the ropes and make it move like a pendulum. Then take the other end of the rope and grab the scissors as they come toward you. Then tie the knot.

187. By gradually pouring sand into the hole. The bird will keep moving so that it is not buried in the sand, forcing it higher until it comes out.

188. He makes three cigarettes out of the nine cigarette butts. Every time he smokes one cigarette, he has one new cigarette butt. In total, he smokes four cigarettes and, therefore, smokes for four hours.

189. Cut it either of these ways:

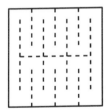 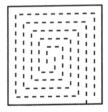

190. In two dimensions there is no solution, but it is possible in three dimensions, where you can form a tetrahedron.

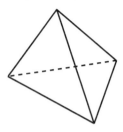

191. Oil floats in vinegar. All you have to do is to tilt the bottle. To pour vinegar, you have to turn the bottle upside down and by pulling off the cork a little, you can let the desired amount of vinegar out.

192. By placing it diagonally in a 30-by-30-inch package.

193. Cross your arms and hold a tip of the napkin in each hand. When you uncross your arms, the knot will be formed.

194. Yes, very easily, by folding the paper and then wrinkling it as shown below.

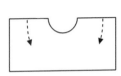 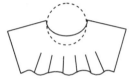

195. Make a knot with a loop at the base of the rope, and then cut the loop. The knot will be still holding the ends of the rope.

196. First, tie the lower ends. Then climb up the first rope and cut the second one, close to the ceiling, leaving an end long enough to form a loop. (You can instead cut it off entirely if you can slide the rope through the hook.) Hanging from the loop, cut the first rope at the hook. Be careful not to drop it. Then slide the rope through the loop until it's even. Climb down the double rope and, once on the floor, pull one end to get it all.

197. Pour water in the hole a little at a time. The ball will rise until it completely comes out of the hole.

198. By releasing some air from the tires so that they lower the total height of the truck more than two inches. The truck can then easily go under the bridge.

199. By tossing it upward. First it will go up, then it will stop momentarily and start coming down following the same path.

200. By cutting the wood into two or three pieces, 20 centimeters in length. In this way, you obtain pieces with a rectangular surface of 5 by 20 centimeters and you can then put them in the hole, stopping the leak.

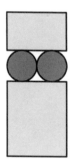 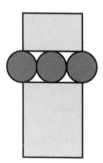

201. Yes, by putting on your pants inside-out.

202. When you take off your shoe, I'll take off mine at the same time. That way, you are not doing it alone.

203. By pushing the cork inside the bottle.

204. By turning the box upside down and sliding the lid enough to make some diamonds fall. Then close it, turn it back to its original position, and put it back in its place.

205. The paper reads, "You will write the word 'NO' on the paper." If you write "NO," you are indicating that it will not happen, although it has really happened. If you write "YES," you are indicating that it will happen, although it actually has not happened. No matter what you write, you will not get it right.

206. Save one penny every other day. When he dies, you will have the exact amount.

207. Place the newspaper page under a closed door. Each person steps on one end of the page so that they cannot touch each other without opening the door. To open the door, they would have to step off of the paper.

208. Something that specifically involves you. For example, crawling under your legs. Your friend can crawl under your legs, but you cannot crawl under your own legs.

209. Roll up the rug (or the bill) starting on one end until it reaches the bottle. Then, continue rolling it slowly so that the bottle moves until it is entirely off the rug. During this process, only the rug is touching the bottle.

210. Always advance half the distance remaining to the wall. In this way, there will always be some distance between you and the wall. The distance left approaches zero, but it never actually reaches zero.

If we consider d as the initial distance to the wall, the distance traveled is $d \times (\frac{1}{2} + \frac{1}{4} + \frac{1}{8} + \frac{1}{16} + \ldots + \frac{1}{2^n})$.

211. Because they placed the ballpoint pen on the ground leaning against a high wall.

212. To make the authorities think that he was going to jump with a hostage. If they thought that, they would not give him a defective parachute.

213. There were no footprints. Therefore, the man and package fell from the sky. The package was the parachute that had not opened up. That is why the man was dead.

214. He was on a long bridge, so he had to run 20 yards toward where the police car was approaching from to get off the bridge. Then he ran toward the forest.

215. The husband died before he woke up. Therefore, nobody could have known what he had been dreaming about.

216. The man used the ladder to tie the rope to the hook. Then, he took it out of the room and brought in a big block of ice. He stood on the block of ice to hang himself. The moisture on the floor came from the ice melting down.

217. He talked to the travel agency where the couple had bought their tickets and found out that the husband had ordered a one-way ticket for his wife and a round-trip ticket for himself.

218. He took out one marble and swallowed it before someone else could see its color. This forced the count to take out the other marble. It was black, of course, so they all assumed that the previous one had been white.

219. He dug up the dirt with his hands to form a little mound. He then stepped on the mound to reach the water.

220. The man stabbed himself with an icicle. The ice melted. This explains why there was no weapon.

221. If Albert had stopped the cassette player when the killer came in, the tape would not have been rewound. This means that the killer had listened to the tape to make sure that the imitation was perfect.

222. The killer blocked the deadbolt with a chunk of ice. When the ice melted down, the door locked itself.

223. The maid, because pages 99 and 100 are two sides of the same sheet of paper.

224. If the police detective heard the shots at the same time, it means that the men could not have died at the same time. If both sounds had occurred at the same time at opposite ends of the train, he would have first heard the one from the front car, because the speed of the train was added to the speed of sound. For the sound from the back of the train, the speed of the train was subtracted from the speed of sound. For the detective to hear both shots at once means the man at the back of the train was killed first.

225. The guilty man was one Siamese twin, and his twin was innocent.

226. New York City is in the Northern Hemisphere and Australia is in the Southern Hemisphere. Due to the earth's movement, water and air masses turn in different directions in both hemispheres. In the Southern Hemisphere, they turn clockwise, while in the Northern Hemisphere, they turn counterclockwise. When he saw the direction of the water draining from the sink, he knew where he was.

227. The footprints were not very deep, which means that they could not belong to a very heavy person. Therefore, they had to belong to the secretary, who had changed shoes to hide her crime.

Both wounds must have occurred when the victim placed a hand on his chest before the gunshot and the bullet crossed his hand before going into his chest.

228. I climbed up a cherry tree that had two cherries and picked only one. I left the other one on the tree. I did not "pick cherries," because I "picked a cherry."

229. Humans. When we are little, we crawl on all fours. When we are adults, we stand on two feet. When we are old, we use a cane.

230. Silence.

231. The letter "i."

232. A shadow.

233. None. The ship floats and it always weighs the same in the water. It will rise with the tide, so its flotation line will always be the same. So the ladder will still be 22 steps.

234. Two minutes. During the first minute, the front of the train will pass through the tunnel and during the second minute, the rest of the train will pass through the tunnel.

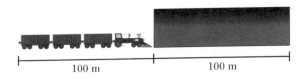

100 m   100 m

235. When they crossed, they were both in the same place. Therefore, they were both equidistant from Madrid.

236. The trains going to the movies arrive one minute earlier than the other ones. So if my uncle arrives at a random time, nine times out of ten the movie train will come first.

237. Two hours and thirteen minutes. (If you multiply by 60, the minutes become hours and the seconds become minutes.)

238. If you put my bird inside any supersonic plane and make it fly in the same direction as the plane, it will be going faster than the plane.

239. The top of the highest mast in the boat traveled a distance 2πd feet longer than the lowest point of the boat, which is d feet lower.

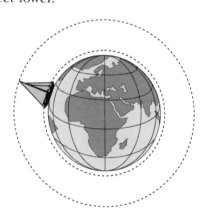

240. A bird cannot fly on the moon because there is no air to suspend it.

241. The passenger should sit at the end of the train and when the train enters the tunnel, he should run toward the front of the train. The time he spends in the tunnel will be shorter than if he had remained seated.

242. The combined speed of the trains is 50 + 70 = 120 miles per hour. It will take them half an hour to travel the 60 miles between them. During this time, the bird will travel 40 miles.

243. 100 inches. The stone moves relative to the log and the log to the terrain.

244. The combined speed of the trains is $80 + 120 = 200$ meters per minute. One minute before crashing, they will be 200 meters apart.

245. You might think that the snail would take 200 minutes in traveling 100 centimeters, but you have to realize that at the end of the 194th minute it will be three centimeters away from the end. This means that in the 195th minute, the snail will reach it and will not slide down again. The answer is 195 minutes.

246. The young man took ten minutes to go to the other end of the train and back. During this time, the man's suitcases have traveled five miles. The train travels five miles every ten minutes, which makes the speed 30 miles per hour.

247. Fifteen, counting the times that they meet at a port while one ship is leaving and the other arriving. Thirteen, if we do not count these crossings. When the ship leaves, there are already seven ships on the way that it will come across at some point during the journey. It will also cross with the one ship that leaves when it leaves and the seven other ships that will depart during the ship's journey. The figure below represents this situation. The arrow indicates a ship that leaves New York destined for London. The dotted lines indicate the ships it passes.

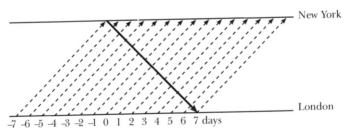

248. The needle will travel approximately 9.5 centimeters (the radius of the record minus the non-playable areas, $15 - 5 - 0.5 = 9.5$ centimeters.) Actually, the speed of the record and the number of grooves do not affect the result. The needle moves in an arc of a circle whose radius is the length of the tonearm.

249. This point maintains a constant speed, independent of the length of the shadow.

250. When the car speeds up, the inertia pushes the air back inside the car, compressing the air behind the balloon and thus pushing the balloon forward. When the car turns, the balloon will move toward the inside of the turn.

251. The lower ends of the rim of the wheels. Their trajectory is shown below:

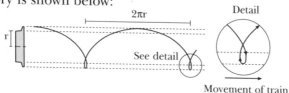

When the train goes in one direction, those points move in the opposite direction.

252. If the dog went faster than 330 meters per second (the speed of sound), it could not hear the noise of the can. So that is the fastest the dog can run.

253. Because the speed ratio was the same, runner number "1" won. We can verify this mathematically:

$v/v_2 = 100/95 = 105/x_2$

$x_2 = 99.75$ meters

254. The director got to the office 20 minutes early and he saw the car at "x" distance from his house. Then the car takes 20 minutes in traveling that distance back and forth. So the director came across the car 10 minutes before his regular departure time and therefore he walked exactly 50 minutes.

255. Without the current, the boat takes 20 minutes. It goes six miles in twenty minutes, so its speed is 18 mph.

With a current, the first trip would be $V_1 = 18 - 2 = 16$ mph, taking $T_1 = D/V_1 = 3/16 = 11$ minutes and 15 seconds. The return trip would be $V_2 = 18 + 2 = 20$ mph, taking $T_2 = 3/20 = 9$ minutes.

The total trip, in this case, would take 20 minutes and 15 seconds, which is more than the trip without the current.

Quick-to-Solve Brainteasers

256. There is such a spot. Let's imagine that on the same day that one person was climbing down, the other one was climbing up. They must have met at a certain point of the trip. This is the spot we are looking for.

257. Two blankets one inch thick each, because the air between them also acts as insulation.

258. No. It hasn't because the total weight of the ice is equal to the volume of water moved.

259. This can never happen. These are two contradictory concepts. If one of them exists, the other cannot possibly exist as well.

260. At the North or South Pole.

261. I must pour it before going upstairs, because the coffee will lose more heat before adding the milk rather than after. (Matter loses heat proportionally to the difference in temperature with the surrounding environment.)

262. The flotation line will be lower, because the raft will be lighter. The water level of the pool will also be lower, because the volume of water that the rocks move when they are in the raft is larger than the volume of water the rocks move when they are at the bottom of the pool. When the rocks are on the raft, they move a volume of water equal to the weight of the rocks. When the rocks are at the bottom of the pool, the volume of the water moved is equal to the actual volume of the rocks. Since rocks are denser than water, this is the smaller of the two volumes.

263. The flotation line will be the same, because the weight of the boat does not change.

264. Eight times, as shown below.

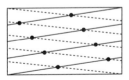

265. While the raft is loaded with the salt, he must mark the flotation line. Then, he must unload the salt and load the raft with gold until the water level reaches the flotation line. This means that the weight of the salt and the gold will be equal.

266. Place the bottle horizontally and let the wine gradually pour out until the horizontal surface of the wine is at the middle of the bottle, as shown in the illustration.

267. Put pieces of glass of the broken pitcher in the pitcher containing acid until the level reaches the five-quart mark. Then pour the acid until it reaches the two-quart mark.

268. Before leaving home, he wound the clock and set it for 12:00. When he got back home, he knew exactly how long he had been out because of his own clock.

At his friend's house, he checked the time. Once he was back home, he subtracted the time he was at his friend's house from the total time indicated by the clock. The remainder was used in walking to and from his friend's house. He divided this number into two and added the result to the time that he saw on his friend's clock when he was leaving his friend's house.

269. Two turns on itself. (You can actually try this yourself.)

270. Mr. Brown does not wear a brown or white tie. Therefore, it has to be red. Mr. White's tie can't be white, so it must be brown. That leaves Mr. Red with the white tie.

271. The maximum distance for the first two points is when they are on opposite ends of a circumference of that sphere. The circumference divides the sphere in two hemispheres. The third point has to be in one of these hemispheres. Therefore, it will certainly happen.

272. The puzzle says to draw a square "with two straight lines." The easiest solution is the one shown in the illustration below, which shows a square with two straight lines.

273. It is possible to predict it. That doesn't mean that he is right in his predictions.

274. This puzzle is based on an old joke. What really happened was that the young man kissed his own hand and then slapped the older man in the face.

275. There is no smoke coming out of an electric train.

276. Peacocks don't lay eggs. Peahens do.

277. A hole, for example.

278. One dozen.

279. He has a glass eye.

280. A quintet.

281. When he got married, he was a billionaire. Because of his wife's spending habits, he became a millionaire.

282. He can take out his dentures and bite his good eye with them.

283. Baby elephants.

284. During his last lap.

285. You can go in through the door.

286. The hare was lying. (The first paragraph of the puzzle gives the order.)

287. Staying up at night.

288. Wet.

289. Bicycles.

INDEX

Numbers refer to puzzle numbers.

WHAT IS AMERICAN MENSA?

AMERICAN MENSA
The High IQ Society

One out of 50 people qualifies
for American Mensa ...
Are YOU the One?

American Mensa, Ltd. is an organization for individuals
who have one common trait: a score in the top two percent
of the population on a standardized intelligence test. Over
five million Americans are eligible for membership ... you
may be one of them.

• Looking for intellectual stimulation?
You'll find a good "mental workout" in the *Mensa Bulletin*, our
national magazine. Voice your opinion in the newsletter published by your local group. And attend activities and gatherings with fascinating programs and engaging conversation.

• Looking for social interaction?
There's something happening on the Mensa calendar
almost daily. These range from lectures to game nights to
parties. Each year, there are over 40 regional gatherings
and the Annual Gathering, where you can meet people,
exchange ideas, and make interesting new friends.

• Looking for others who share your special interest?
Whether your interest might be as common as computer
gaming or as esoteric as eugenics, there's probably a Mensa
Special Interest Group (SIG) for you. There are over 150
SIGs, which are started and maintained by members.

So contact us today to receive a free brochure and application.

American Mensa, Ltd.
1229 Corporate Drive West
Arlington, TX 76006
(800) 66-MENSA
AmericanMensa@compuserve.com
http://www.us.mensa.org

If you don't live in the U.S. and would like to get in touch with your national Mensa, contact:

Mensa International
15 The Ivories
6-8 Northampton Street, Islington
London N1 2HY England